AMERICAN KENNEL CLUB

Puppy Love!

Giant Coloring & Activity Book

© 2010 American Kennel Club, Inc.
AKC, American Kennel Club
and the trademarks, logos and
designs are trademarks of
the American Kennel Club, Inc.

Modern Publishing
A Division of Unisystems, Inc.
New York, New York 10022
Printed in the U.S.A
Series UPC: 49255

We love to play!

1.

TIME FOR A TREAT

Help the puppy get to the bone by following the correct path through the maze.

See Answers

Will you be my friend?

2.

MAN'S BEST FRIEND

Dogs make great pets and are loyal companions. Do you have a dog? Write all about it! If you don't have your own dog, write about a favorite dog that you know!

1.

2.

3.

4.

3.

DOGGY DIFFERENCES

Circle the dog that looks different from the rest!

See Answers

Playing in the park is fun!

I'm sleepy!

Dinnertime!

4.

A FAVORITE PLACE

Connect the dots from 1 to 12 and see where a dog can go when it wants to be alone!

See Answers

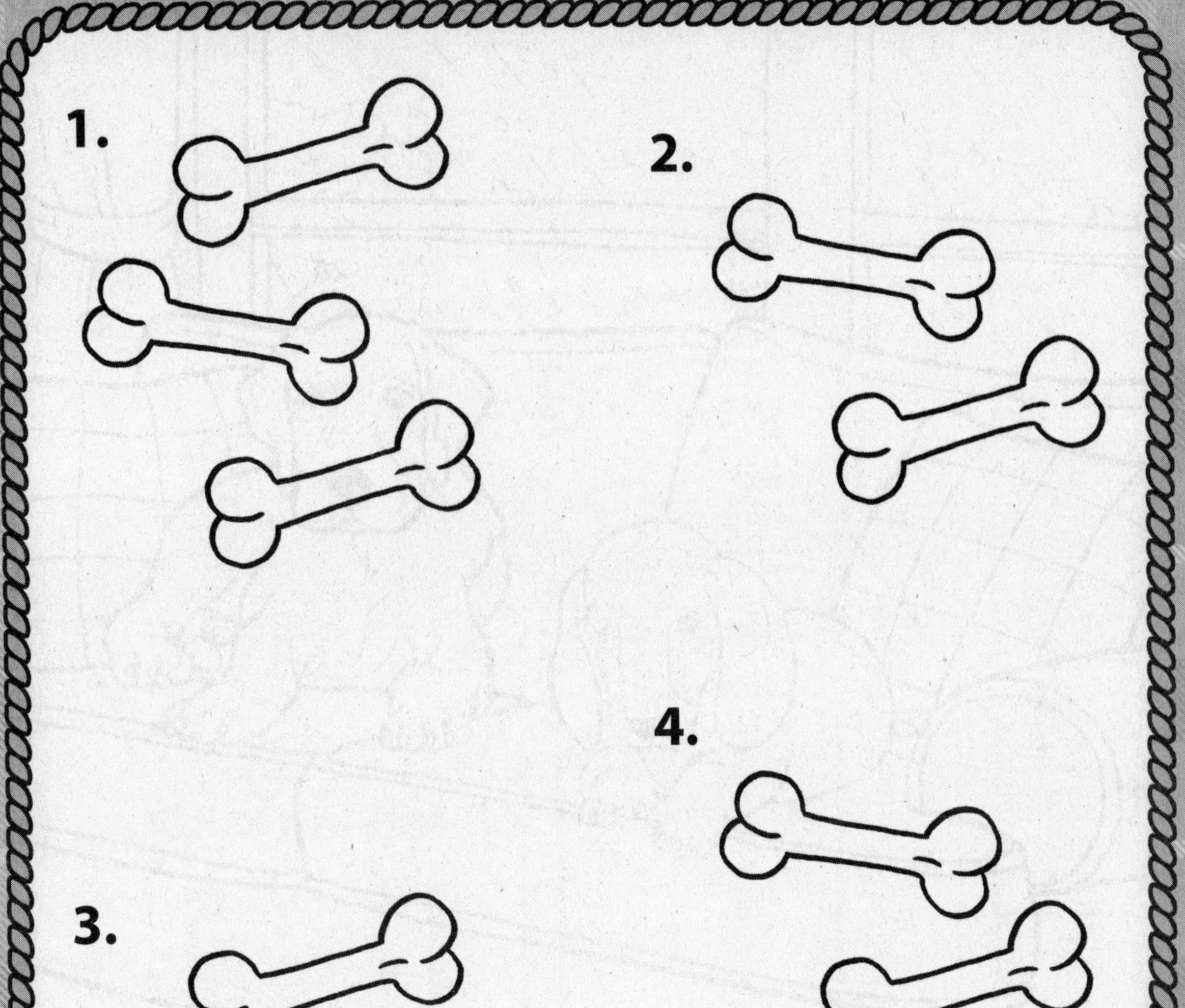

5.

HOW MANY BONES?

Look at each picture.
Circle the picture that has five dog bones.

See Answers

We don't like rainy days!

What's over there?

A G B L E E

____

6.

NAME THAT DOG BREED!

Unscramble the letters to spell out the name of the breed of this dog!

See Answers

Can we go for a walk?

Let's go for a ride!

7.

IDENTICAL DOGS

Look at the pictures.
Draw lines to match each dog to its twin.

See Answers

I'm going this way!

PUPPY 101

Do you wish that you could have your very own puppy? Puppies are fun, loving and playful—but they are also a big responsibility. Before you ask your parents if you can have a dog, here's what you'll need to know.

• Puppies come in all shapes and sizes. Do you have a favorite breed? If you do, research it at the library or go online. Will your choice be a good fit for your family? Smaller dogs, like Chihuahuas, need less exercise and are good choices if you live in an apartment and do not have a backyard. Larger dogs, like Labrador Retrievers, can grow very large and need lots of outdoor activity. After you've done your research, sit down with your family and tell them what you've learned. You'll be one step closer to having a new companion!

• A new puppy can be a big expense. They will need visits to the vet and basic necessities like a crate for housebreaking, food, a collar and leash, and medicine. Not to mention toys!

•Is your family very busy and hardly ever home? Puppies need a lot of attention and care, and will need someone to be home with them a good amount of the time.

• Puppies need to be trained properly in order to become happy members of a home. They will need to be housebroken and taught basic commands. Training puppies takes a lot of patience, but it's worth it!

• No matter what the weather, puppies will need to be walked often (after they have received all of their proper vaccinations from the vet, of course!). Be prepared to walk your puppy—anytime of day!

• If you've given having your own puppy a lot of thought and it's a responsibility you are willing to accept, congratulations! Dogs are wonderful companions and will bring lots of love to you and your family!

C	U	D	D	L	E	Z	X	T	B
Y	C	E	B	L	P	L	A	Y	X
Y	N	B	E	W	M	I	Y	O	P
P	M	C	H	P	E	L	S	A	P
P	X	H	T	U	W	R	U	N	U
Y	A	B	V	Y	U	I	T	M	W
H	T	N	N	D	Y	I	U	A	P
S	T	R	E	T	C	H	U	I	E

Eat **Run**
Play **Nap**
Stretch **Cuddle**

8.

DOG DAYS

Find the words in the grid that describe what dogs love to do! Look up, down, across and diagonally!

See Answers

We're out of treats?

9.

BRAND NEW COLLAR

Which puppy is not wearing a collar? Circle it!

See Answers

I love my new toy!

We have so much fun at the dog run!

10.

BEST FRIENDS

How many three-letter and four-letter words can you make from the phrase MAN'S BEST FRIEND? Write the words on the lines.

See Answers

I think it's time for a bath!

Look what I found!

May I have a biscuit?

We love to play in the snow!

Let's race!

We love the lake!

11.

D IS FOR DOG

Dog starts with the letter D.

What other things on this page start with the letter D?

Circle them!

See Answers

We're waiting for our owner.

We love the beach!

HOUSEBREAKING HELPERS

Need tips on how to housebreak your new puppy? These pointers will help you teach your dog everything he'll need to know!

Crate-training your puppy is a great way to housebreak him. Dogs think of a crate as their home and do not like to get it dirty, so they will do their best to avoid having an accident in it. Make your puppy's crate comfortable by putting in a comfy dog bed and his favorite toy. Cover the crate with a fluffy blanket to help mimic the "den" atmosphere that puppies like.

- Use the crate for naps and for when your puppy sleeps at night. A puppy should not be kept in a crate all day long, and it should not be used for punishment.

- Your new puppy should be taken outside approximately every two hours. If your puppy has just finished eating or playing, take your puppy out immediately. Most puppies will give you a signal when they have to go, like barking, whining, or pacing back and forth.

- It helps to feed your puppy and take him outside at the same times each day. Puppies like to have a schedule—it makes learning easier!

- When your puppy goes to the bathroom outdoors, give him lots of praise! He will learn that certain actions will reap rewards—like hugs, kisses or treats!

- If your puppy has an accident in the house, scold him gently but firmly. Do not punish your puppy. Mistakes happen!

Let’s go on a hike!

12.

COUNT THE SPOTS!

Count the number of spots on the Dalmatian and write your answer on the line!

See Answers

I love to cuddle!

Home Sweet Home

FRONT

13.

DOGGY PAD!

Color and cut out this fun mouse pad!

BACK

Peek-a-Boo!

Let's go this way!

Sleep Tight!

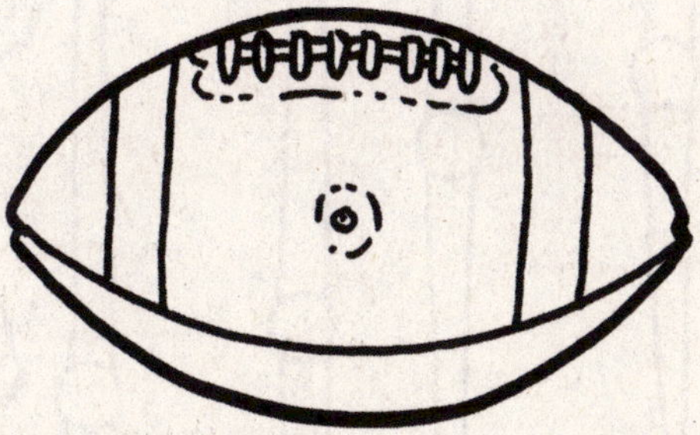

14.

DINNERTIME!

This puppy is hungry!
Underline what he'll have for dinner.

See Answers

You can do it!

15.

GOOD MORNING!

Which puppy is still sleeping? Circle it!

See Answers

We love going for walks!

U L B G D L O

____

16.

SECRET CODE

Unscramble the letters to spell out the name of this lovable dog breed!

See Answers

I want to play outside!

Let’s play!

17.

SNACK TIME!

This puppy is hungry!
Draw some treats that you think it will like!

Can you help me find my favorite toy?

18.

MY FAVORITE DOG

What does your favorite dog look like?
Draw it here!

Best in Show

I hear a noise!

19.

FUN WITH WORDS

How many three-letter and four-letter words can you make from the words GREAT DANE? Write them on the lines above.

See Answers

1=Green
2=Brown
3=Yellow
4=Blue

20.

COLOR BY NUMBER

Color the picture using the color code in the box.

What a pretty flower!

PUPPY'S FIRST YEAR

Read all about what to expect in your puppy's first year of life!

8 to 12 Weeks

Puppies are very curious at this age! But they can also be fearful of their environment and loud sounds, so try to provide a quiet home for your puppy. Their permanent teeth are starting to grow in, so make sure you have lots of chew toys for them to play with!

A puppy's immune system doesn't fully develop until they're 12 weeks old. Therefore, your dog will need to get all of his "puppy shots" at the vet before he can be around other dogs or walk on the ground outside. (Your puppy is very susceptible to germs at this age and needs all of his shots so he doesn't get sick from anything that he finds on the ground.)

Since your puppy can't walk on the ground outside, they will need a place where they can go to the bathroom. Make sure you put out extra housebreaking pads around the house!

Your puppy is growing very fast! Young puppies at this age will have to eat four times a day. But don't give your puppy "people" food—they should stick to vet-recommended food only.

Playtime is important, but so is naptime! Play with your puppy for only a few minutes at a time, as they will need their rest afterwards.

You can start teaching your puppy how to wear a collar, walk on a leash and come to you when you call his name. Keep these training sessions to only a few minutes at a time, and don't forget to give your puppy lots of praise with hugs and kisses!

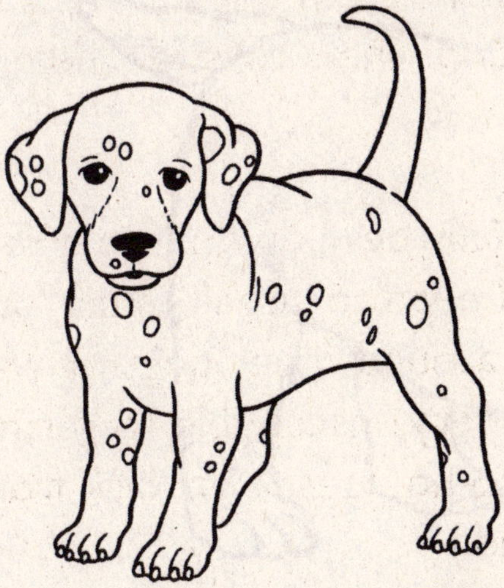

12 to 16 Weeks

Housetraining can now really begin, since at this age, your puppy will have had all of his shots and can now be walked outside. Make sure to take your puppy on frequent walks throughout the day!

When your puppy is four months of age, he is in what's called the "critical socialization period." How your puppy acts during this time will foreshadow what your puppy will be like as an adult dog. Your puppy needs the most nurturing at this age—he will need fun experiences, positive interactions with other people and animals, and praise when he comes when called, fetches a toy or goes to the bathroom outside.

Now is the time that your puppy will have to start taking medicine to prevent heartworm disease. Make sure to schedule a visit to the vet!

Reduce feedings from four times a day to three.

4 to 6 Months

Puppies at this age experience an "avoidance period" and will be wary of new experiences, situations and places. Your puppy will look to you for support so make sure you provide plenty of reassurance! But don't force them to interact with other dogs or other situations that may make them uncomfortable. Gently encourage your puppy and don't be pushy.

Talk to your vet about spaying or neutering your puppy and whether your puppy should take a monthly flea and tick medication.

Puppies experience a growth spurt during this time, so make sure to check that your dog's collar isn't too tight.

6 to 9 Months

Puppies need lots of exercise during these three months! Make sure to take your puppy on lots of walks and engage him in lots of playtime.

Reduce the number of feedings to twice a day.

To keep your puppy out of mischief when he's in the house, try to keep him with you as much as possible. Try to teach him to stay with you and lie beside you when it's time for him to rest. Remember, the more exercise your puppy has outside, the more tired he will be in the house.

9 to 12 Months

Some puppies experience separation anxiety during this time. Make sure you greet your puppy enthusiastically when you come home, and give him lots of kisses and hugs before you leave the house!

Your puppy should still be eating twice a day, but if you notice that they are gaining too much weight, cut back on their food intake a little bit. Check with your vet to see if your puppy is eating the proper amount of food for their age and size.

Give yourself a pat on the back and give your puppy a kiss! Your healthy, happy puppy is having a birthday soon!

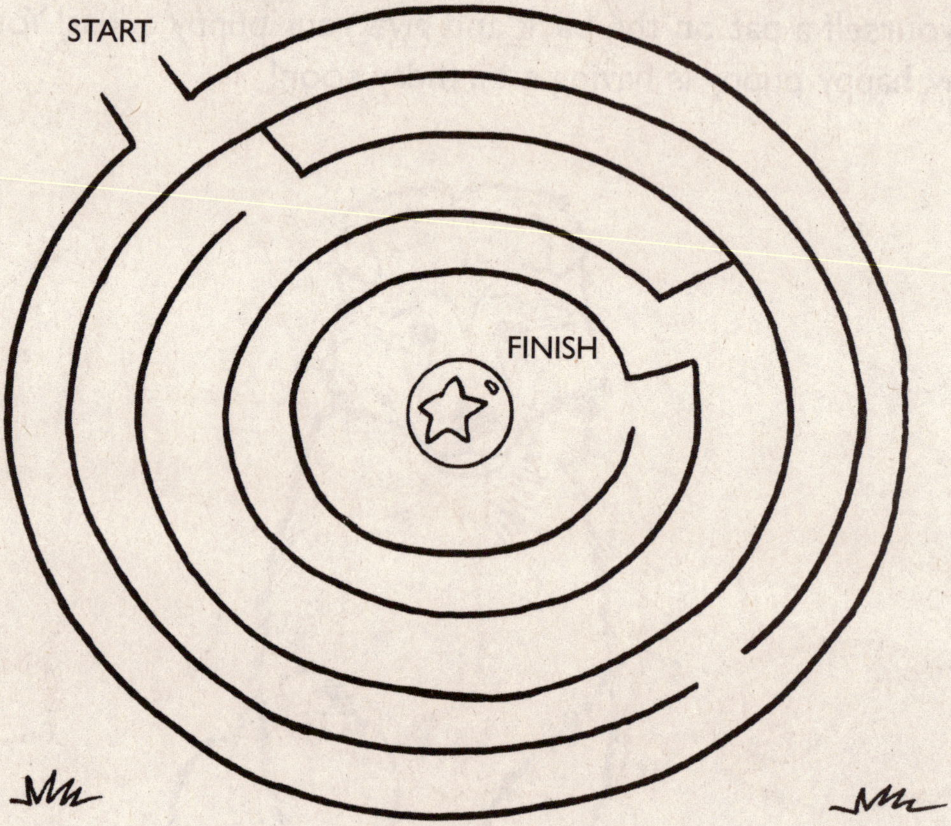

21.

WHERE'S THE BALL?

Help the puppy get to his ball by following the correct path through the maze.

See Answers

We are best friends!

1.

2.

3.

4.

22.

FANCY COLLARS

Circle the collar that looks different from the rest!

See Answers

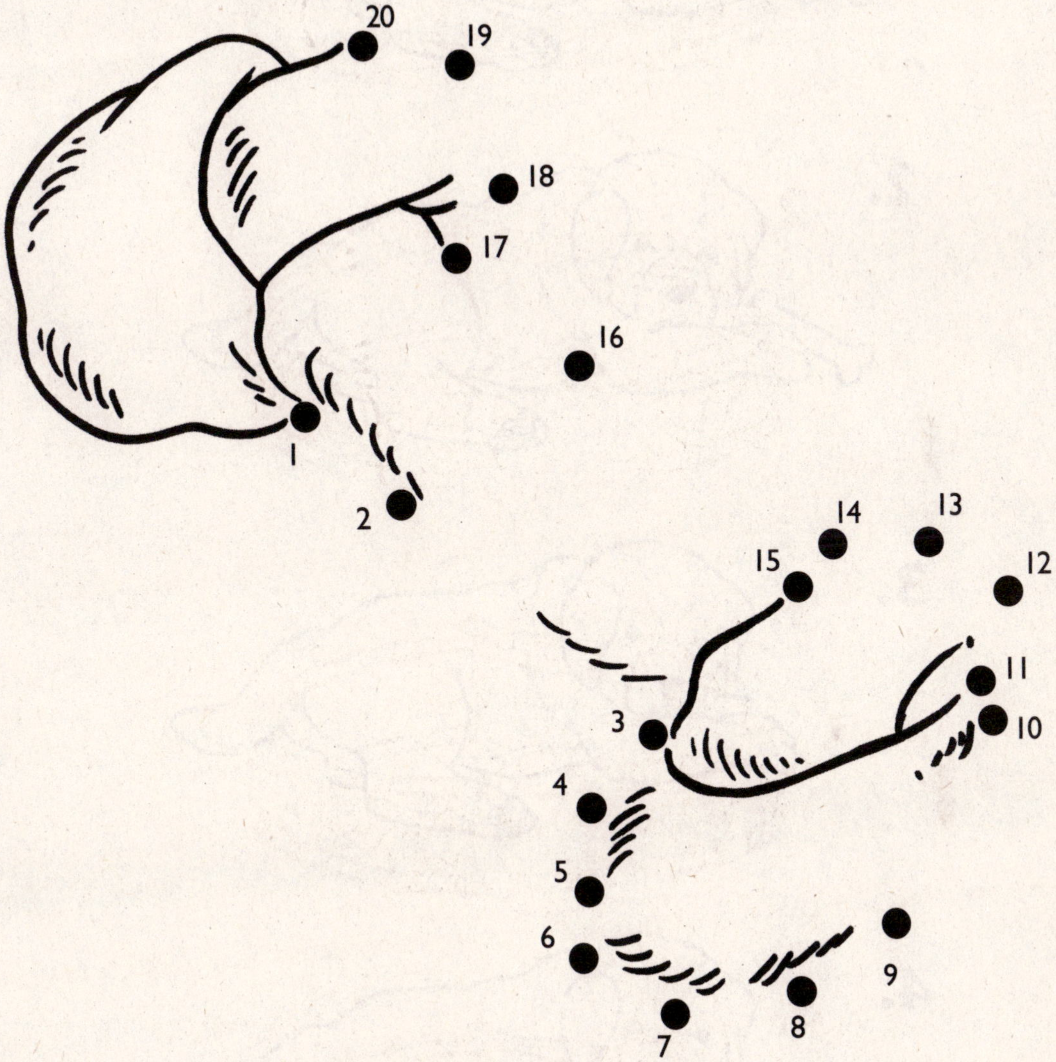

23.

DOG TREATS

Connect the dots from 1 to 20 to see a dog's favorite treat!

See Answers

1.

2.

3.

4.

24.

GIVE A DOG A BONE

Which puppy doesn't have a bone? Circle your answer!

See Answers

I love you!

BOY **BONE**

TREAT

SUN **JOY**

25.

RHYMING WORDS

How many words rhyme with the word "toy?"
Circle your answers!

See Answers

1.

2.

3.

4.

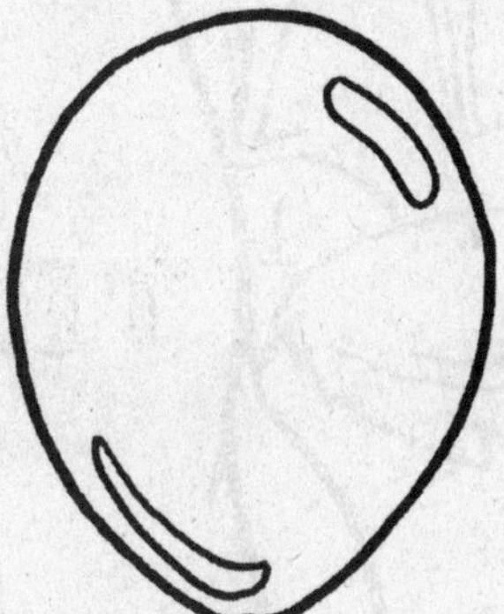

26.

FIND THE DOGS

A Westie is a type of dog. What other dogs are in the picture? Circle them!

See Answers

27.

COLOR BY NUMBER

Color the scene by using the color code in the box.

1=Black	5=Blue
2=Brown	6=Pink
3=White	7=Green
4=Yellow	8=Red

See you in the morning!

ANSWERS

1.

3.

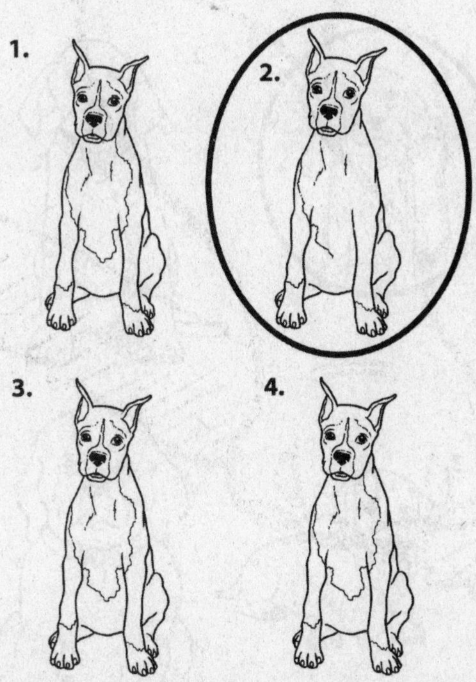

4.

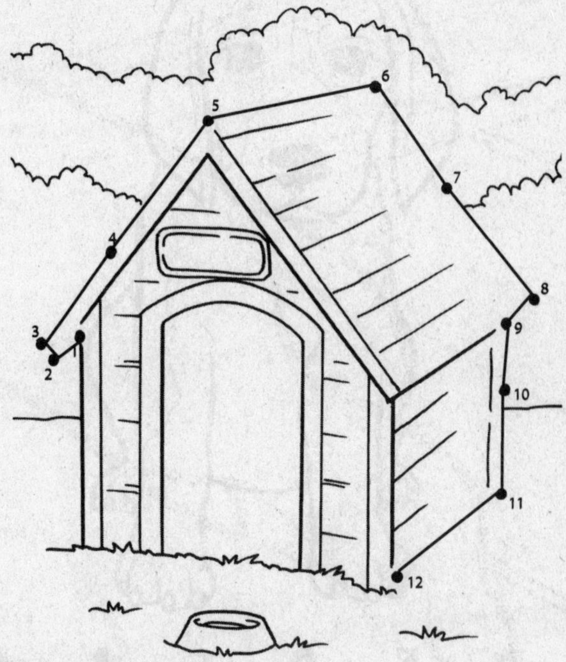

5.

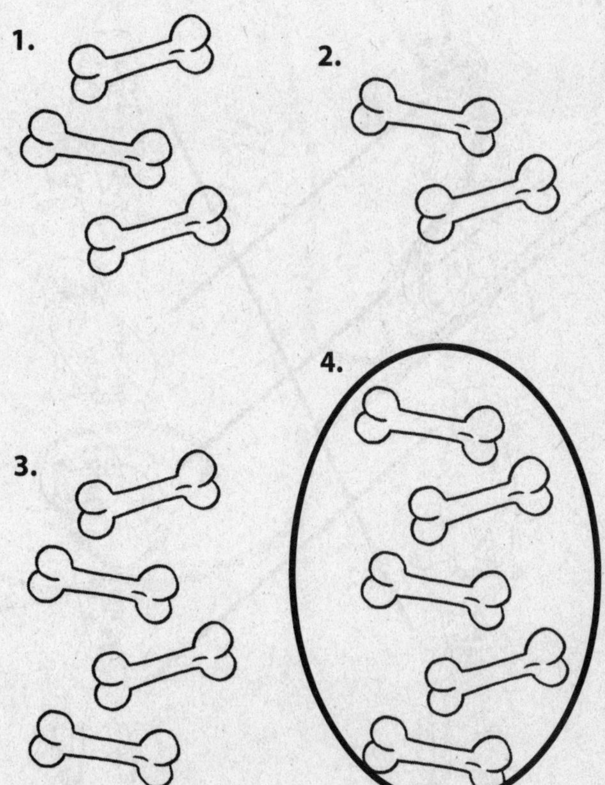

ANSWERS

6.

B E A G L E

8.

C	U	D	D	L	E	Z	X	T	B
Y	C	E	B	L	P	L	A	Y	X
Y	N	B	E	W	M	I	Y	O	P
P	M	C	H	P	E	L	S	A	P
P	X	H	T	U	W	R	U	N	U
Y	A	B	V	Y	U	I	T	M	W
H	T	N	N	D	Y	I	U	A	P
S	T	R	E	T	C	H	U	I	E

7.

9.

ANSWERS

10.

SOME POSSIBLE ANSWERS ARE:

TEAM	SAND
FIND	BIT
TEA	TAN

12.

19

11.

14.

ANSWERS

15.

16.

B U L L D O G

19.

SOME POSSIBLE ANSWERS ARE:

TAG	RAG
GATE	TAR
TREE	RENT
NET	NEAT

ANSWERS

21.

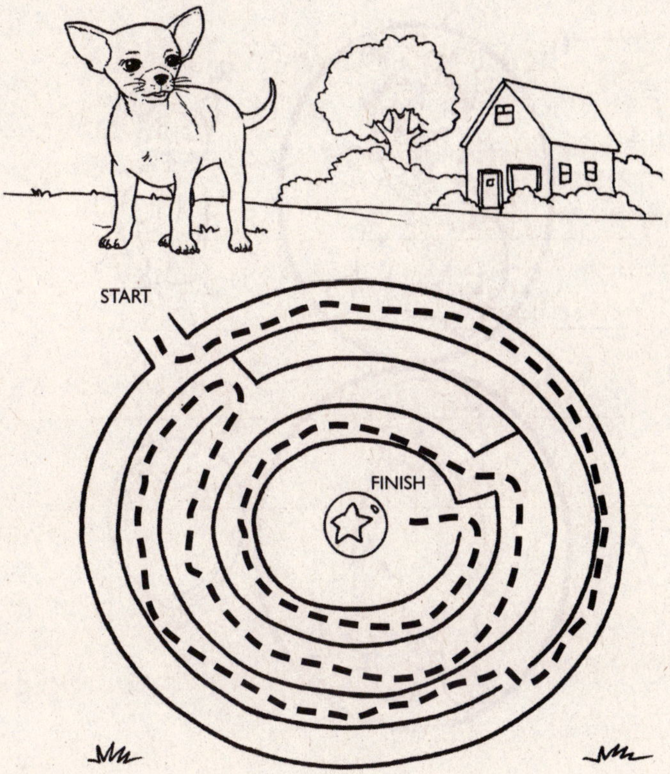

22.

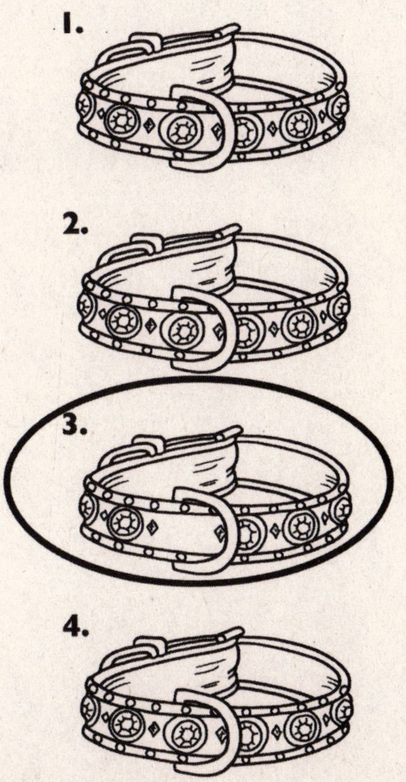

23.

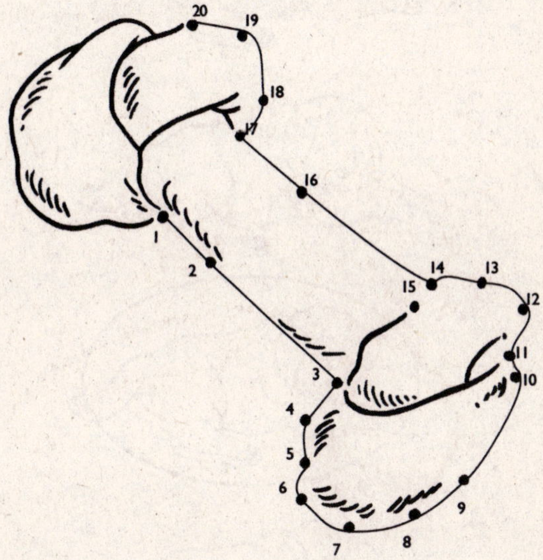

ANSWERS

24.

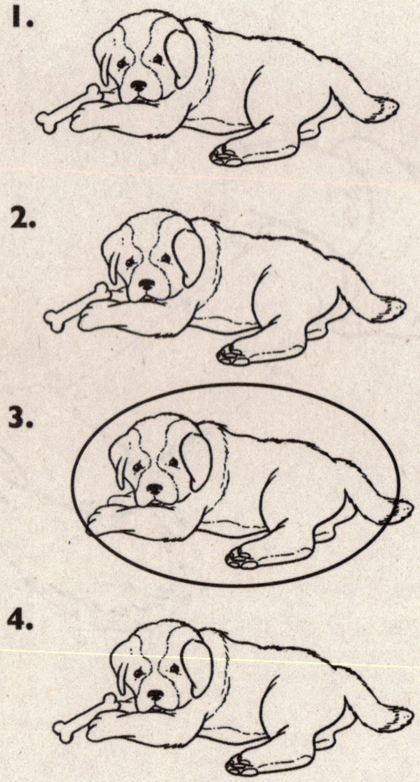

26.

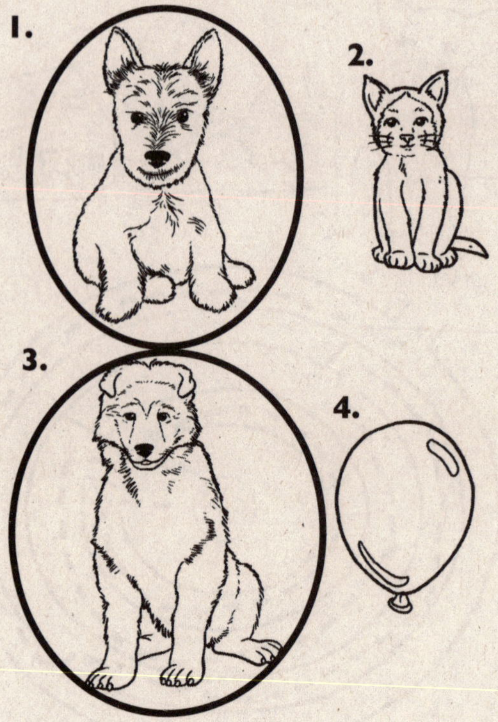

25.

BOY **BONE**

TREAT

SUN **JOY**